For Bette Rypke

All Good Wishes
Love
Ashley Bryan
'80

I
GREET
THE DAWN

Poems by
Paul Laurence Dunbar

I
GREET
THE DAWN

Poems by
Paul Laurence Dunbar

Selected, Illustrated,

and with an Introduction by

Ashley Bryan

Love Ashley Bryan

ATHENEUM · NEW YORK

1978

To the memory of my nephew
CHARLIE
1959–1977
"I greet the dawn and not a setting sun
When all is done."

Library of Congress Cataloging in Publication Data

Dunbar, Paul Laurence, 1872–1906.
I greet the dawn.

SUMMARY: A brief biography of the poet precedes a
collection of his works, most in standard English rather
than dialect, with such themes as love, hate, death,
nature, and religion.
[1. American poetry—Afro-American authors]
I. Bryan, Ashley. II. Title.
PS1556.A2B7 1978   811'.4   77–21232
ISBN 0–689-30613–X

Published simultaneously in Canada by
McClelland & Stewart, Ltd.
Manufactured in the United States of America by
The Halliday Lithograph Corporation
West Hanover, Massachusetts
Typography by Mary M. Ahern
First Edition

CONTENTS

I
GREET
THE DAWN

Poems by
Paul Laurence Dunbar

Paul Laurence Dunbar

At the turn of the century, one of America's most famous writers was the black poet, Paul Laurence Dunbar. He was born on June 27, 1872, in Dayton, Ohio, the son of former slaves. He was of the first generation of blacks born into freedom in the United States.

Dunbar's mother, Matilda Glass, had been married as a slave to Willis Murphy and had two sons by him, born into slavery. Willis and Matilda Murphy were from different plantations in Kentucky. Under slavery, they were forced to live apart but after the Civil War the family lived together briefly before Willis Murphy died.

The widowed Matilda Murphy then moved to Dayton, Ohio, with her sons to join her mother and grandmother who had settled there many years earlier. It was there that she met Joshua Dunbar, who was twenty years her senior. They were married in 1871.

Joshua Dunbar had escaped from slavery in Kentucky by means of the Underground Railroad. He fled to freedom in Canada, but returned to the States during the Civil War to fight for the freedom of his people.

Joshua and Matilda Dunbar worked hard to support their family. In the evenings they studied to become literate. This right had been denied them by law under slavery, but now they learned to read and to write. They also agreed that their son, Paul, would have an education. They taught him the alphabet, and when he was of age, they entered him in the public school.

Paul was twelve years old when his father died. His step-brothers, who had dropped out of school to work, moved to Cincinnati and then on to Chicago to seek better jobs, and his mother became his sole support. She took in laundry so that Paul could stay in school, and Paul helped her after school.

In Central High School, Paul Laurence Dunbar was the only black in his class. His poems began to appear in school and local newspapers and he became known as a writer. He was admitted to the school's literary society and, in his senior year, was elected president of this society and editor of the school paper.

Despite frail health, Paul was an active youngster. After school, when he was not helping his mother, he and his friends did any odd jobs they could find to earn pocket money and they often talked of their plans for the future. Among them was Paul's close friend, Bud Burns, who went on to medical school and later became private physician to his poet friend.

An all-black minstrel troupe came to a theatre in town and Paul and his friends went to the performance. Paul was so excited by the event that he formed his own drama group. He wrote skits and cast his friends in the parts. The amateur troupe was much in demand for church and social fund-raising affairs.

Dunbar wrote the lyrics for the class song, which were set to music by the music teacher and sung at the commencement exercises. After graduating from high school, he would have liked to attend college but this was out of the question. His mother had worked hard to see him through high school, and he wished to make things easier for her now.

He tried to find a job that would relate to his skills and interests and stimulate his growth as a writer. His schoolmates, Orville and Wilbur Wright, had begun a newspaper, and Dunbar often stopped at the printing office to chat with them. Dunbar started his own small newspaper for the black community, which the Wright brothers printed for him, but the venture failed. So Dunbar had to look to the large established businesses in town for a chance to earn a living and apply his talents. However, despite his reputation in the community, no office or newspaper job was open to him. The ads stated, "No colored boy need apply."

Dunbar finally got a job running an elevator in a downtown building. He kept a notebook handy on the job and between calls jotted down ideas and worked on poems. He learned the poetic forms by studying the works of the great poets, and he felt especially close to the English poets Tennyson, Keats and Shelley. They inspired him to shape his joy and sorrow into verse of a lyric intensity that brought him release from the limitations of his job.

In the summer of 1892, the Western Association of Writers met in Dayton, Ohio. One of Dunbar's former teachers served on the committee for this event. She remembered Dunbar's gifts as a writer and invited him to prepare a welcoming address for the Association.

Dunbar put a lot of time and thought into this address, which he decided to deliver entirely in verse. He was able to get just enough time from his job to give the speech. He read his poem, and the audience of writers responded enthusiastically. Dunbar then hurried back to his post on the elevator.

Many of the writers inquired about this talented black youth, and they went to find him at his job as elevator boy. One of the writers, Dr. James Matthews, was especially interested in the young poet. He rode the elevator with him up and down, questioning him and asking for poems that he could use in a newspaper article.

Dr. Matthews invited Dunbar to become a member of the Western Association of Writers and to read from his work the following day. When he returned to the Convention the writers gave him a standing ovation and his reading was a great success.

The article that Dr. Matthews wrote on his return home to Mason, Illinois, was printed in many newspapers throughout the country. Dunbar's most treasured response to this article was a letter he received from the famous poet James Whitcomb Riley who addressed him as "my chirping friend" and wrote "your gift . . . is a superior one." Dunbar was encouraged by this letter and by the praise of the writers at the meeting. He decided to select from his work and publish a book of his poems.

In late December of 1892 Paul Laurence Dunbar's first book of poetry *Oak and Ivy* was published. It was through the kindness of William L. Blocher, the business manager of the United Brethren Publishing House in Dayton, that this became possible.

William Blocher had read Dunbar's poems in the town newspapers and thought highly of Dunbar's work. He offered to help him. Dunbar accepted Blocher's advance of one hundred and twenty-five dollars in order to see his book in print. At his salary of four dollars a week, this sum represented more than half a year's earnings, a considerable risk for the young poet.

Fortunately, the book had strong local support from Paul's friends at the African-Methodist-Episcopal Church, which he and his mother attended, from friends at Central High School and from townspeople. Dunbar also sold copies to customers on the elevator. Within two weeks he was able to repay the advance. Fourteen years later Dunbar dedicated *Joggin' Erlong,* a book of his selected verse in dialect to William Blocher, who had made publication of the first book possible.

Oak and Ivy came to the attention of two men in Toledo, Ohio, an attorney, Charles Thatcher, and Dr. H. A. Tobey. They invited Dunbar to give talks in Toledo, and when they met him were impressed with his character and abilities.

Throughout his life these men remained among Dunbar's closest friends. They recognized the sensitive qualities of the young poet, and they believed in his gifts. Both men took an active interest in promoting Dunbar's career and helped him in times of critical financial need.

The publication of *Oak and Ivy* gave Paul and his mother great satisfaction, but it in no way relieved their financial condition. In 1893 Dunbar left for the World's Columbian Exposition in Chicago, hoping to find a better job there. He did a number of odd jobs before meeting the black leader Frederick Douglass who was commissioner in charge of the Haitian exhibit.

Frederick Douglass praised Dunbar's poetry and encouraged the ambitions of the young poet. He hired Dunbar as his clerical assistant and paid him five dollars a week out of his own pocket. On Colored Americans' Day at the Fair, Dunbar sat on the platform with Douglass and other notables before thousands of people gathered in Festival Hall. After Douglass gave his speech, Dunbar read his poetry. The audience responded warmly and was even more enthusiastic when informed that the verse was his own. Douglass later inscribed one of his books to Dunbar: "From Frederick Douglass to his dear young poet friend Paul Dunbar, one of the sweetest songsters his race has produced and a man of whom I hope great things." The tribute poems that Dunbar wrote after the death of Frederick Douglass in 1895 were based on his personal relationship with this great man.

The Exposition ended, and Dunbar returned to Dayton and to his old job as elevator boy. The extremely limited opportunities for making a living discouraged Dunbar at times. It seemed he could never make ends meet. Yet he could write to Dr. Tobey in June of 1895, "Yes, I am tied down and have been by menial labor, and any escape from it so far has been only a brief respite that made the return to drudgery doubly hard. But I am glad to say that for the past two or three years I have been able to keep my mother from the hard toil by which she raised and educated me. But it has been and is a struggle."

In 1896 Dunbar's second book of poetry *Majors and Minors* was published by the Hadley & Hadley Printing Company in Toledo, Ohio. His friends Dr. Tobey and Mr. Thatcher had put up the money for this publication. It was through Dr. Tobey's connections that this book was given to the influential novelist and critic William Dean Howells, who wrote a highly favorable review of it in an issue of *Harper's Weekly.* The interest stirred by this review brought Paul Laurence Dunbar national attention and acclaim.

William Dean Howells enthusiastically praised Dunbar's dialect poems in *Majors and Minors,* but he minimized the poems in standard English. He expanded on the verse that made him feel ". . . in the presence of a man with a direct and fresh authority to do the kind of thing he is doing." Apparently that "authority" meant dialect and did not carry over to the other poems. He wrote ". . . I do not think one can read his Negro pieces without feeling that they are of like impulse and inspiration with the work of Burns when he was most Burns, when he was most Scotch, when he was more peasant. When Burns was least himself he wrote literary English, and Mr. Dunbar writes literary English when he is least himself."

This opinion of Dunbar's work set a line of criticism that haunted and distressed the poet throughout his life.

Dunbar himself did not speak in dialect, nor did those closest to him. However, he discovered in dialect an important outlet for his lively wit and love of characterization. He had a good ear and listened carefully to those whose speech he interpreted in his dialect pieces. He was able to utilize the dramatic possibilities that dialect gave him as well, and this added to the popular appeal of his public readings.

There was, however, much more of himself that Dunbar wished to communicate through his poems. He grew up hearing his parents' stories of what it was like under slavery.

His father had told of his escape from slavery and of his return to fight with the black Fifty-Fifth Regiment, the second regiment of blacks recruited in the North.

His mother had told the story behind her coming to Dayton, Ohio, to live. An abolitionist, Samuel Steele, who acted on his anti-slavery principles, bought Matilda Dunbar's grandmother. He brought her to his hometown of Dayton, Ohio, settled her there and freed her.

Matilda's mother had also been freed by her owner, but only so that he could be rid of the expense of supporting her. She had become too old to be of further use to him.

Dunbar's mother had told him of the painfulness of the

forcible separation from her first husband and the fear that her own children could be sold away from her.

These stories were a vital part of Dunbar's life. Furthermore, he grew to maturity during a crucial period in America's history. The post Civil War legislation, designed to assure equal citizenship rights for the freedmen, were often difficult to enforce, and economic and social discrimination against blacks was extreme.

Dunbar knew these pressures, and he also recognized the many white people who actively helped him. There were the teachers and school friends and townspeople in Dayton who had encouraged his gifts as a writer, the business manager who had made publication of his first book possible, the patrons who invited him to give readings and who stood by him when he was refused hotel accommodations when reservations had been made well in advance, the doctor and attorney in Toledo, Ohio, who were always ready to help him. The interest and support of these people led, at times, to conflict with the established prejudices of others, but Dunbar's friends didn't give in.

Dunbar had a need to express the tensions and contradictions that these experiences aroused. The humorous stance that he generally took in the dialect pieces did not allow for this. He knew that minstrel shows had conditioned his audience to expect laughter and comfortable sentiments in this genre, so he rarely used dialect for a direct statement of serious themes. These themes and the moods they evoked he transformed into eloquent English verse. He believed in these poems and indicated his sense of their relation to the dialect poems by the titles of his privately published books, *Oak and Ivy, Majors and Minors.*

Following William Dean Howells' review of *Majors and Minors,* Paul Laurence Dunbar accepted a contract offer from Dodd, Mead and Company in New York. In 1896 they published

Dunbar's *Lyrics of Lowly Life.* This volume of one hundred and five poems was made up of twenty poems from *Oak and Ivy,* seventy-four from *Majors and Minors* and eleven new poems.

The wide distribution of this major publishing house made Dunbar's poetry available to a national audience. Howells wrote the introduction in the same vein as his *Harper's Weekly* review. He praised the dialect poems highly, writing, "In nothing is his essentially refined and delicate art so well shown as in these pieces . . ." Of Dunbar's poems in standard English Howells wrote, "Some of these I thought very good, and even more than very good, but not distinctively his contribution to the body of American poetry."

There was no escape for Dunbar from Howells' judgment. As the introduction to *Lyrics of Lowly Life* it exerted an influence that extended to the criticism of Dunbar's three other books of poetry published before his death. It appears today as the introduction to the book of Dunbar's complete poems and continues to inhibit a broader response to Dunbar's poetry.

Lyrics of Lowly Life proved very popular, and for many years sold thousands of copies a year, most unusual for a book of poetry. Dunbar's reputation grew, and there was an increasing demand for his work.

He had always been interested in all kinds of literature, and he now began writing short stories, novels, articles and essays. There were many requests from newspapers for articles, and Dunbar said to a friend: "The age is materialistic. Verse isn't. I must be with the age. So, I am writing prose."

However he always came back to his center, poetry. He immersed himself in writing, hoping to earn enough to support himself and his mother and to realize his plans for marriage.

Dunbar had been struck by a poem and a photograph of

Alice Ruth Moore that had appeared in a journal. He wrote her, and they corresponded for over two years. Alice Moore was a college graduate who had dedicated herself to teaching children. She and Dunbar met and became engaged in 1897 just before Dunbar left the States for a reading tour of England.

In England, Dunbar gave readings of his work and met other writers. John Hay, the American ambassador, introduced him to the black English composer, Samuel Coleridge-Taylor, and arranged a joint recital for them. The composer set a number of Dunbar's poems to music and the program was presented with Coleridge-Taylor playing for the singers and Dunbar reading from his verse.

The musical quality of Dunbar's verse has often been noted, and Coleridge-Taylor was only one of the composers to set the poems to music. Dunbar later collaborated with the black composer Will Marion Cook on a musical that became a Broadway hit, *Clorindy or The Origin of the Cakewalk*. Despite the show's success, Dunbar felt uneasy with the black stereotype of the minstrel show, and he resisted Cook's efforts towards further collaboration. However he relented later and wrote some of the most popular lyrics for Cook's musical *In Dahomey*. This show took the cakewalk abroad and created such a sensation in London that it played a command performance at Buckingham Palace.

Dunbar enjoyed being in England but the reading tour was poorly organized. Finally his manager deserted him, and he was left stranded in London. Still, Dunbar used the time to advantage, writing stories, poems and most of his first novel, *The Uncalled*. But this did not help his financial plight. He exhausted all means of staying on or raising money to return and eventually had to write to his friend Dr. Tobey who cabled the money to come home.

Dunbar returned from England in the fall of 1897 to a job as assistant in the reading room of the Library of Congress. The salary gave him the security he needed to suggest marriage to his fiancee. He and Alice Ruth Moore were married in 1898 the year in which *The Uncalled,* dedicated to his wife, and his first book of short stories *Folks from Dixie,* dedicated to Dr. Tobey, were published. She left her work as a teacher in New York and joined Paul and his mother at their home in Washington, D.C.

Dunbar especially enjoyed the library sessions when he read to children and gave other readings. However much of his time was spent in the dusty book stacks behind the iron gratings among books on medicine and the natural sciences. "I am in love with literature (he wrote to a friend) and wish I could give my whole time to reading and writing, but alas! one must eat, and so I plod along, making the thing that is really first in my heart, secondary in my life . . ." The job offered him a steady income, but it proved damaging to his health. Dunbar had never been very strong and now the inhalation of dust among the book stacks irritated his lungs, causing the onset of tuberculosis.

His wife, hearing his cough in the night, planned vacations to get him away to fresh air and sunshine in the country. Dunbar loved fishing, and their trips took them to rivers and the sea. In an essay on her husband's poetry "The Poet and His Song" she wrote, "To the soul born inland, the sea is always a revelation, and a wonder-working experience in the life. . . . When the sea became a part of the poet's life, it wrapped itself naturally into his verse—but hardly ever disassociated from the human element. . . . Narragansett Pier had opened his eyes to the mystic beauty of the ocean, and his soul to its turbulence. The journey to England made him familiar with the gray nothingness of mid-ocean, and life subsequently meant frequent pilgrimages to the seashore. Gray skies and gray sea; these meant most to him; sombreness and gloom seemed part of the real meaning of the ocean. One need not seek in the life of the poet a kinship between love of the serious aspects of nature and a fancied wrong or injury in life. . . . A poet is a poet because he *understands;* because he is born with a divine kinship with all things, and he is a poet in direct ratio to his power of sympathy."

After a year and a half Dunbar, encouraged by his wife, decided to leave his job at the Library of Congress and try to earn his living by his writing and by filling speaking engagements offered him. He was very much in demand as a reader and traveled extensively reading from his poetry. His poems were written with an ear for the exact rhythm and beat. He had a rich baritone voice and the reviews often noted that he was "one of the few writers who could read well." For Dunbar, himself, there was always a special delight in experiencing the direct response of the audience to his readings.

Reading aloud gave Dunbar a chance to emphasize the lyric qualities of his verse. He could convey the subtle rhythms of his work in the vocal rendering of a phrase. Then, too, his voice could illumine a line that, on the printed page, escaped meaning, or bring grace to a passage that had seemed awkward.

Dunbar took advantage of as many of these public readings as he could fill. At the invitation of Booker T. Washington, he visited Tuskegee Institute several times and lectured to the English classes. He also stopped to read at other schools and colleges along the way. However, the effects of the accumulation of dust in his lungs weakened him, and in the spring of 1899, on his way to a reading in Albany, New York, where he was to be introduced by Governor Theodore Roosevelt, he collapsed in New York

City with fever and racking coughs. An attack of pneumonia brought him close to death, but after a month he rallied.

Dunbar recovered sufficiently to continue his writings, but his public appearances were drastically curtailed. His lungs were impaired by the illness and he wrote in a letter, "I am often despondent, for it is hard to sing in the dark. But I find that two of the sweetest songbirds—the nightingale and the mockingbird —do the same." He and his family first moved to the Catskills in hopes of a complete recovery in a more favorable environment. The landscape surprised him with fresh images of nature, which he described in his poems. But his lungs did not heal well enough, so the doctor prescribed the high, dry climate of Colorado; and the family moved there, settling in Harmon, near Denver.

Dunbar here regained some of his former strength, but he drove himself hard to meet the many assignments he had accepted, as well as to advance his own work. Though pressured to produce, his standards remained high. When asked about his methods of composition, he said, "Indeed, my work becomes harder, rather than easier, as I go on, simply because I am more critical of it. I believe when an author ceases to climb, he ceases at the same time to lift his readers up with him."

Dunbar's spirits rose and fell with his illness. From Colorado he wrote to a friend: "I too have looked upon the 'little red hair-like devils' who are eating up my lungs. So many of us are cowards when we look into the cold, white eyes of death, and I suppose I am no better or braver than the rest of humanity." Still he courageously pursued his aims as a writer, and his books of poetry, short stories and novels were published regularly.

Colleges awarded him honorary degrees. He was elected to the American Social Science Association for distinction in literature, and invitations of all kinds were extended to him. He was given the honorary rank of Colonel for the Inaugural Parade of President McKinley in 1901 and rode horseback in the procession. When Vice-President Theodore Roosevelt became President after the assassination of President McKinley, Dunbar was among those at the White House New Year's Day reception and President Roosevelt greeted him warmly.

As a result of Dunbar's publications, there was a steady flow of invitations, but he generally was too ill to accept. Sometimes his visitors had to be restricted. The chest pains continued and Dunbar often hemorrhaged. As his health began to fail, his mother, who was a strong woman and very close to her son, gave him all the care and attention that he needed. His wife also faced the challenge with courage. As a poet, essayist and short story writer, she had much in common with her husband. She understood his work and supported his aims. She loved him and did all she could, but neither of them could control the severe strains placed on their marriage by Dunbar's ill health, the constant moving, the financial problems and the conflicting needs of mother and wife. In January of 1902, Paul and Alice Dunbar separated.

The quarrel that led to the separation was slight, but it hid unspoken grievances, and the result was serious. Dunbar's mother was in Chicago at the time, visiting her older sons for the holidays. Alice and Paul both wrote to her seeking her sympathy. "Write to me," Alice begged Ma Dunbar. "I'll be faithful to you. We have been through enough to stick together until the end of time." But at that distance, there was nothing the mother could do to help.

Had the plea sent to the mother been sent to Paul, the hurt

would have been forgiven, but pride and anger kept them both from taking the steps that would reunite them. Months passed before Paul wrote to Alice, and then she refused to see him. In despair Dunbar wrote to a friend, "I am greatly discouraged, and if I could do anything else, I should give up writing. Something within me seems to be dead. There is not spirit or energy left in me."

Dunbar found his voice again through poems of love and sorrow and continued writing and publishing through these difficult years. His health declined steadily, and his last two years were spent almost as an invalid. His childhood friend Bud Burns had become a doctor and was now his private physician. He came daily and nursed Dunbar through the many crises of his illness. Then suddenly, unexpectedly, in November of 1905, Dr. Burns died. It was a tremendous blow to Dunbar. He insisted on attening the funeral and went to the cemetery as well. There he stood shivering in the cold, stunned by the loss of his dear friend.

Dunbar was now too weak to write, so he dictated his thoughts to a friend. His lungs and throat were ravaged by tuberculosis, but he still sought to capture the lines of poetry that flickered through his mind. He knew he was in a fighting race with death and had written earlier, "If this is to be so, I feel like pulling my horse, and letting the white rider go in without a contest." But as the New Year approached he said expectantly, "I am lying fallow. I believe my soil has become greatly impoverished, but it will take a good many more rains and snows to put anything into it worth coming out in blossom."

A month later, on February 9, 1906, Paul Laurence Dunbar died in his home in Dayton, Ohio, at the age of 33 with his mother attending him to the end.

During his lifetime Paul Laurence Dunbar never saw a selection of his poetry that focused on his poems in standard English. from 1899 to his death in 1906, six volumes of selected poems appeared. Each book was handsomely produced, with photographs illustrating the poems and decorative borders framing each page. These volumes were made up almost entirely of the dialect poems.

There is today a volume of selected poems designed to introduce his work to young people. It is again confined to a selection of his dialect poems.

Dunbar had at first accepted Howells's personal view of his poems, and he had thanked him by letter and in person for all that the review had done for his career. In his many readings, Dunbar enjoyed the response of audiences, black and white, to his dialect poems, but he also noted the audience's deep response to his poems in standard English. He therefore hoped for greater critical appreciation of his poetry in this vein.

When it was not forthcoming he wrote to a friend, "One critic says something and the rest hasten to say the thing, in many cases using the identical words. I see now very clearly that Mr. Howells has done me irrevocable harm in the dictum he laid down regarding my dialect verse."

The statement was severe but it emphasized Dunbar's need for a more open response to his range as a poet. "I'm tired of dialect" he said, "but the magazines aren't. Everytime I send them something else, they write back asking for dialect. Nothing wrong with the poems—a Dunbar just has to be dialect, that's all." It was this narrowness of attitude that Dunbar resisted. He overcame it whenever he shaped a dialect poem out of honest emotion and conviction, and he refused to let it overwhelm his need to touch roots with his natural voice, which he tapped in over two-thirds of his verse.

In Alice Dunbar's essay about her husband's poetry, published after his death, she wrote: "Say what you will, or what Mr. Howells will, about the 'feeling the Negro life esthetically, and expressing it lyrically,' it was in the pure English poems that the poet expressed *himself*."

The purpose of this selection is to offer Paul Laurence Dunbar's poetry in standard English with a few of the dialect poems. This presentation may then lead the reader to discoveries that take into account more of his poems in the language in which he thought, in the English that reflected his natural way of speaking.

To that aim Dunbar himself would surely say: "Amen!"

BECAUSE
YOU LOVE ME

ENCOURAGED

Because you love me I have much achieved,
Had you despised me then I must have failed,
But since I knew you trusted and believed,
I could not disappoint you and so prevailed.

LOVE'S HUMILITY

As some rapt gazer on the lowly earth,   2 3
    Looks up to radiant planets, ranging far,
So I, whose soul doth know thy wondrous worth
    Look longing up to thee as to a star.

LONGING

If you could sit with me beside the sea to-day,
And whisper with me sweetest dreamings o'er and o'er;
I think I should not find the clouds so dim and gray,
And not so loud the waves complaining at the shore.

If you could sit with me upon the shore to-day,
And hold my hand in yours as in the days of old,
I think I should not mind the chill baptismal spray,
Nor find my hand and heart and all the world so cold.

If you could walk with me upon the strand to-day,
And tell me that my longing love had won your own,
I think all my sad thoughts would then be put away,
And I could give back laughter for the Ocean's moan!

ALICE

Know you, winds that blow your course
   Down the verdant valleys,
That somewhere you must, perforce,
   Kiss the brow of Alice?
When her gentle face you find,
Kiss it softly, naughty wind.

Roses waving fair and sweet
   Thro' the garden alleys,
Grow into a glory meet
   For the eye of Alice;
Let the wind your offering bear
Of sweet perfume, faint and rare.

Lily holding crystal dew
   In your pure white chalice,
Nature kind hath fashioned you
   Like the soul of Alice;
It of purest white is wrought,
Filled with gems of crystal thought.

Seen my lady home las' night,
  Jump back, honey, jump back.
Hel' huh han' an' sque'z it tight,
  Jump back, honey, jump back.
Hyeahd huh sigh a little sigh
Seen a light gleam f'om huh eye,
An' a smile go flittin' by—
  Jump back, honey, jump back.

Hyeahd de win' blow thoo de pine,
  Jump back, honey, jump back.
Mockin'-bird was singin' fine,
  Jump back, honey, jump back.
An' my hea't was beatin' so,
When I reached my lady's do',
Dat I couldn't ba' to go—
  Jump back, honey, jump back.

Put my ahm aroun' huh wais',
  Jump back, honey, jump back.
Raised huh lips an' took a tase,
  Jump back, honey, jump back.
Love me, honey, love me true?
Love me well ez I love you?
An' she answe'd, " 'Cose I do"—
  Jump back, honey, jump back.

BALLAD

I know my love is true,
  And oh the day is fair.
The sky is clear and blue,
The flowers are rich of hue,
  The air I breathe is rare,
  I have no grief or care;
For my own love is true,
  And oh the day is fair.

My love is false I find,
  And oh the day is dark.
Blows sadly down the wind,
While sorrow holds my mind;
  I do not hear the lark,
  For quenched is life's dear spark,—
My love is false I find,
  And oh the day is dark!

For love doth make the day
  Or dark or doubly bright;
Her beams along the way
Dispel the gloom and gray.
  She lives and all is bright,
  She dies and life is night.
For love doth make the day,
  Or dark or doubly bright.

INVITATION TO LOVE

Come when the nights are bright with stars
    Or when the moon is mellow;
Come when the sun his golden bars
    Drops on the hay-field yellow.
Come in the twilight soft and gray,
Come in the night or come in the day,
Come, O love, whene'er you may,
    And you are welcome, welcome.

You are sweet, O Love, dear Love,
You are soft as the nesting dove.
Come to my heart and bring it rest
As the bird flies home to its welcome nest.

Come when my heart is full of grief
    Or when my heart is merry;
Come with the falling of the leaf
    Or with the redd'ning cherry.
Come when the year's first blossom blows,
Come when the summer gleams and glows,
Come with the winter's drifting snows,
    And you are welcome, welcome.

IF

If life were but a dream, my Love,
    And death the waking time;
If day had not a beam, my Love,
    And night had not a rhyme,—
A barren, barren world were this
Without one saving gleam;
I'd only ask that with a kiss
You'd wake me from the dream.

If dreaming were the sum of days,
    And loving were the bane;
If battling for a wreath of bays
    Could soothe a heart in pain,—
        I'd scorn the meed of battle's might,
        All other aims above
        I'd choose the human's higher right,
        To suffer and to love!

LOVE'S APOTHEOSIS

Love me. 1 care not what the circling years
    To me may do.
If, but in spite of time and tears,
    You prove but true.

Love me—albeit grief shall dim mine eyes,
    And tears bedew,
I shall not e'en complain, for then my skies
    Shall still be blue.

Love me, and though the winter shall pile,
    And leave me chill,
Thy passion's warmth shall make for me, meanwhile,
    A sun-kissed hill.

And when the days have lengthened into years,
    And I grow old,
Oh, spite of pains and griefs and cares and fears,
    Grow thou not cold.

Then hand and hand we shall pass up the hill,
    I say not down;
That twain go up, of love, who've loved their fill,—
    To gain love's crown.

Love me, and let my life take up thine own,
    As sun the dew.
Come, sit, my queen, for in my heart a throne
    Awaits for you!

OVER THE HILLS

Over the hills and the valleys of dreaming
   Slowly I take my way.
Life is the night with its dream-visions teeming,
   Death is the waking at day.

Down thro' the dales and the bowers of loving,
   Singing, I roam afar.
Daytime or night-time, I constantly roving,—
   Dearest one, thou art my star.

LOVE

A life was mine full of the close concern
   Of many-voiced affairs. The world sped fast;
   Behind me, ever rolled a pregnant past.
A present came equipped with lore to learn.
Art, science, letters, in their turn,
   Each one allured me with its treasures vast;
   And I staked all for wisdom, till at last
Thou cam'st and taught my soul anew to yearn.
   I had not dreamed that I could turn away
From all that men with brush and pen had wrought:
   But ever since that memorable day
When to my heart the truth of love was brought,
   I have been wholly yielded to its sway,
And had no room for any other thought.

THOU ART MY LUTE

Thou art my lute, by thee I sing,—
   My being is attuned to thee.
Thou settest all my words a-wing,
   And meltest me to melody.

Thou art my life, by thee I live,
   From thee proceed the joys I know;
Sweetheart, thy hand has power to give
   The meed of love—the cup of woe.

Thou art my love, by thee I lead
   My soul the paths of light along,
From vale to vale, from mead to mead,
   And home it in the hills of song.

My song, my soul, my life, my all,
   Why need I pray or make my plea,
Since my petition cannot fall;
   For I'm already one with thee!

34

Pray, what can dreams avail
    To make love or to mar?
The child within the cradle rail
    Lies dreaming of the star.
But is the star by this beguiled
To leave its place and seek the child?

The poor plucked rose within its glass
    Still dreameth of the bee;
But, tho' the lagging moments pass,
    Her Love she may not see.
If dream of child and flower fail,
Why should a maiden's dreams prevail?

SHE GAVE ME A ROSE

She gave me a rose,
    And I kissed it and pressed it.
I love her, she knows,
    And my action confessed it.
She gave me a rose,
    And I kissed it and pressed it.

Ah, how my heart glows,
    Could I ever have guessed it?
It is fair to suppose
    That I might have repressed it:
She gave me a rose,
    And I kissed it and pressed it.

'T was a rhyme in life's prose
    That uplifted and blest it.
Man's nature, who knows
    Until love comes to test it
She gave me a rose,
    And I kissed it and pressed it.

SUPPOSE

If 'twere fair to suppose
   That your heart were not taken,
That the dew from the rose
   Petals still were not shaken,
I should pluck you,
   Howe'er you should thorn me and scorn me,
And wear you for life as the green of the bower.

If 'twere fair to suppose
   That that road was for vagrants,
That the wind and the rose,
   Counted all in their fragrance;
Oh, my dear one,
   By love, I should take you and make you,
The green of my life from the scintillant hour.

LOVE'S PHASES

Love hath the wings of the butterfly,
    Oh, clasp him but gently,
Pausing and dipping and fluttering by
    Inconsequently.
Stir not his poise with the breath of a sigh;
Love hath the wings of the butterfly.

Love hath the wings of the eagle bold,
    Cling to him strongly—
What if the look of the world be cold,
    And life go wrongly?
Rest on his pinions, for broad is their fold;
Love hath the wings of the eagle bold.

Love hath the voice of the nightingale,
    Hearken his trilling—
List to his song when the moonlight is pale,—
    Passionate, thrilling.
Cherish the lay, ere the lilt of it fail;
Love hath the voice of the nightingale.

Love hath the voice of the storm at night,
    Wildly defiant.
Hear him and yield up your soul to his might,
    Tenderly pliant.
None shall regret him who heed him aright;
Love hath the voice of the storm at night.

IN MAY

38

Oh to have you in May,
  To talk with you under the trees,
Dreaming throughout the day,
  Drinking the wine-like breeze,

Oh it were sweet to think
  That May should be ours again,
Hoping it not, I shrink,
  Out of the sight of men.

May brings the flowers to bloom,
  It brings the green leaves to the tree,
And the fatally sweet perfume,
  Of what you once were to me.

SONG

Wintah, summah, snow er shine,
    Hit's all de same to me,
Ef only I kin call you mine,
    An' keep you by my knee.

Ha'dship, frolic, grief er caih,
    Content by night an' day,
Ef only I kin see you whaih
    You wait beside de way.

Livin', dyin', smiles er teahs,
    My soul will still be free,
Ef only thoo de comin' yeahs
    You walk de worl' wid me.

Bird-song, breeze-wail, chune er moan,
    What puny t'ings dey'll be,
Ef w'en I's seemin' all erlone,
    I knows yo' hea't's wid me.

THE POOL

By the pool that I see in my dreams, dear love,
   I have sat with you time and again;
And listened beneath the dank leaves, dear love,
   To the sibilant sound of the rain.

And the pool, it is silvery bright, dear love,
   And as pure as the heart of a maid,
As sparkling and dimpling, it darkles and shines
   In the depths of the heart of the glade.

But, oh, I've a wish in my soul, dear love,
   (The wish of a dreamer, it seems,)
That I might wash free of my sins, dear love,
   In the pool that I see in my dreams.

MORNING SONG OF LOVE

Darling, my darling, my heart is on the wing,
   It flies to thee this morning like a bird,
Like happy birds in springtime my spirits soar and sing,
   The same sweet song thine ears have often heard.

The sun is in my window, the shadow on the lea,
   The wind is moving in the branches green,
And all my life, my darling, is turning unto thee,
   And kneeling at thy feet, my own, my queen.

The golden bells are ringing across the distant hill,
   Their merry peals come to me soft and clear,
But in my heart's deep chapel all incense-filled and still
   A sweeter bell is sounding for thee, dear.

The bell of love invites thee to come and seek the shrine
   Whose altar is erected unto thee,
The offerings, the sacrifice, the prayers, the chants are thine,
   And I, my love, thy humble priest will be.

A MISTY DAY

Heart of my heart, the day is chill,
The mist hangs low o'er the wooded hill,
The soft white mist and the heavy cloud
The sun and the face of heaven shroud.
The birds are thick in the dripping trees,
That drop their pearls to the beggar breeze;
No songs are rife where songs are wont,
Each singer crouches in his haunt.

Heart of my heart, the day is chill,
Whene'er thy loving voice is still,
The cloud and the mist hide the sky from me,
Whene'er thy face I cannot see.
My thoughts fly back from the chill without,
My mind in the storm drops doubt on doubt,
No songs arise. Without thee, love,
My soul sinks down like a frightened dove.

LOVE-SONG

If Death should claim me for her own to-day,
    And softly I should falter from your side,
Oh, tell me, loved one, would my memory stay,
    And would my image in your heart abide?
Or should I be as some forgotten dream,
    That lives its little space, then fades entire?
Should Time send o'er you its relentless stream,
    To cool your heart, and quench for aye love's fire?

I would not for the world, love, give you pain,
    Or even compass what would cause you grief;
And, oh, how well I know that tears are vain!
    But love is sweet, my dear, and life is brief;
So if some day before you I should go
    Beyond the sound and sight of song and sea,
'T would give my spirit stronger wings to know
    That you remembered still and wept for me.

A COQUETTE CONQUERED

Yes, my ha't's ez ha'd ez stone—
Go 'way, Sam, an' lemme 'lone.
No; I ain't gwine change my min'—
Ain't gwine ma'y you—nuffin' de kin'.

Phiny loves you true an' deah?
Go ma'y Phiny; whut I keer?
Oh, you needn't mou'n an' cry—
I don't keer how soon you die.

Got a present! Whut you got?
Somef'n fu' de pan er pot!
Huh! yo' sass do sholy beat—
Think I don't git 'nough to eat?

Whut's dat un'neaf yo' coat?
Look des lak a little shoat.
'T ain't no possum! Bless de Lamb!
Yes, it is, you rascal, Sam!

Gin it to me; whut you say?
Ain't you sma't now! Oh, go 'way!
Possum do look mighty nice,
But you ax too big a price.

Tell me, is you talkin' true,
Dat's de gal's whut ma'ies you?
Come back, Sam; now whah's your gwine?
Co'se you knows dat possum's mine!

A LOVE SONG

Ah, love, my love is like a cry in the night,
A long, loud cry to the empty sky,
The cry of a man alone in the desert,
With hands uplifted, with parching lips,

Oh, rescue me, rescue me,
Thy form to mine arms,
The dew of thy lips to my mouth,
Dost thou hear me?—my call thro' the night?

Darling, I hear thee and answer,
Thy fountain am I,
All of the love of my soul will I bring to thee,
All of the pains of my being shall wring to thee,
Deep and forever the song of my loving shall sing to thee,
Ever and ever thro' day and thro' night shall I cling to thee.
Hearest thou the answer?
Darling, I come, I come.

NIGHT, DIM NIGHT

Night, dim night, and it rains, my love, it rains,
  (Art thou dreaming of me, I wonder)
The trees are sad, and the wind complains,
  Outside the rolling of the thunder,
And the beat against the panes.

Heart, my heart, thou art mournful in the rain,
  (Art thy redolent lips a-quiver?)
My soul seeks thine, doth it seek in vain?
  My love goes surging like a river,
Shall its tide bear naught save pain?

TWILIGHT

'Twixt a smile and a tear,
   'Twixt a song and a sigh,
'Twixt the day and the dark,
   When the night draweth nigh.

Ah, sunshine may fade
   From the heavens above,
No twilight have we
   To the day of our love.

A GOLDEN DAY

I found you and I lost you,
　　All on a gleaming day.
The day was filled with sunshine,
　　And the land was full of May.

A golden bird was singing
　　Its melody divine,
I found you and I loved you,
　　And all the world was mine.

I found you and I lost you,
　　All on a golden day,
But when I dream of you, dear,
　　It is always brimming May.

LOVE'S DRAFT

The draft of love was cool and sweet
   You gave me in the cup,
But, ah, love's fire is keen and fleet,
   And I am burning up.

Unless the tears I shed for you
   Shall quench this burning flame,
It will consume me through and through,
   And leave but ash—a name.

HYMN

O li'l' lamb out in de col',
De Mastah call you to de fol',
O li'l' lamb!
He hyeah you bleatin' on de hill;
Come hyeah an' keep yo' mou'nin' still,
O li'l' lamb!

De Mastah sen' de Shepud fo'f;
He wandah souf, he wandah no'f,
O li'l' lamb!
He wandah eas', he wandah wes';
De win' a-wrenchin' at his breas',
O li'l lamb

Oh, tell de Shepud whaih you hide;
He want you walkin' by his side,
O li'l' lamb!
He know you weak, he know you so';
But come, don' stay away no mo',
O li'l lamb!

An' af'ah while de lamb he hyeah
De Shepud's voice a-callin' cleah—
Sweet li'l lamb!
He answah f'om de brambles thick,
"O Shepud, I's a-comin' quick"—
O li'l lamb!

CONFESSIONAL

Search thou my heart;
   If there be guile,
It shall depart
   Before thy smile.

Search thou my soul;
   Be there deceit,
'T will vanish whole
   Before thee, sweet.

Upon my mind
   Turn thy pure lens;
Naught shalt thou find
   Thou canst not cleanse.

If I should pray,
   I scarcely know
In just what way
   My prayers would go

So strong in me
   I feel love's leaven,
I'd bow to thee
   As soon as Heaven!

ROSES AND PEARLS

52

Your spoken words are roses fine and sweet,
The songs you sing are perfect pearls of sound.
How lavish nature is about your feet,
To scatter flowers and jewels both around.

Blushing the stream of petal beauty flows,
Softly the white strings trickle down and shine.
Oh! speak to me, my love, I crave a rose.
Sing me a song, for I would pearls were mine.

A SONG

Thou art the soul of a summer's day,
Thou art the breath of the rose.
   But the summer is fled
   And the rose is dead;
Where are they gone, who knows, who knows?

Thou art the blood of my heart o' hearts,
Thou art my soul's repose,
   But my heart grows numb
   And my soul is dumb;
Where art thou, love, who knows, who knows?

Thou art the hope of my after years—
Sun for my winter snows;
   But the years go by
   'Neath a clouded sky.
Where shall we meet, who knows, who knows?

Good-night, my love, for I have dreamed of thee
In waking dreams, until my soul is lost—
Is lost in passion's wide and shoreless sea,
Where, like a ship, unruddered, it is tost
Hither and thither at the wild waves' will.
There is no potent Master's voice to still
This newer, more tempestuous Galilee!

The stormy petrels of my fancy fly
In warning course across the darkening green,
And, like a frightened bird, my heart doth cry
And seek to find some rock of rest between
The threatening sky and the relentless wave.
It is not length of life that grief doth crave,
But only calm and peace in which to die.

Here let me rest upon this single hope,
For oh, my wings are weary of the wind,
And with its stress no more may strive or cope.
One cry has dulled mine ears, mine eyes are blind,—
Would that o'er all the intervening space,
I might fly forth and see thee face to face.
I fly; I search, but, love, in gloom I grope.

Fly home, far bird, unto thy waiting nest;
Spread thy strong wings above the wind-swept sea.
Beat the grim breeze with thy unruffled breast
Until thou sittest wing to wing with me.
Then, let the past bring up its tales of wrong;
We shall chant low our sweet connubial song,
Till storm and doubt and past no more shall be!

54

LOVE'S CASTLE

Key and bar, key and bar,
    Iron bolt and chain!
And what will you do when the King comes
    To enter his domain?

Turn key and lift bar,
    Loose, oh, bolt and chain!
Open the door and let him in,
    And then lock up again.

But, oh, heart, and woe, heart,
    Why do you ache so sore?
Never a moment's peace have you
    Since Love hath passed the door.

Turn key and lift bar,
    And loose bolt and chain;
But Love took in his esquire, Grief,
    And there there they both remain.

DAY

The gray dawn on the mountain top
   Is slow to pass away.
Still lays him by in sluggish dreams,
   The golden God of day.

And then a light along the hills,
   Your laughter silvery gay;
The Sun God wakes, a bluebird trills,
   You come and it is day.

THE AWAKENING

I did not know that life could be so sweet,
I did not know the hours could speed so fleet,
Till I knew you, and life was sweet again,
The days grew brief with love and lack of pain—

I was a slave a few short days ago,
The powers of Kings and Princes now I know;
I would not be again in bondage, save
I had your smile, the liberty I crave.

GOOD-NIGHT

The lark is silent in his nest,
    The breeze is sighing in its flight,
Sleep, Love, and peaceful be thy rest.
    Good-night, my love, good-night, good-night.

Sweet dreams attend thee in thy sleep,
    To soothe thy rest till morning's light,
And angels round thee vigil keep.
    Good-night, my love, good-night, good-night.

Sleep well, my love, on night's dark breast,
    And ease thy soul with slumber bright;
Be joy but thine and I am blest.
    Good-night, my love, good night, good-night.

LOVE'S SEASONS

When the bees are humming in the honeysuckle vine
   And the summer days are in their bloom,
Then my love is deepest, oh, dearest heart of mine,
When the bees are humming in the honeysuckle vine.

When the winds are moaning o'er the meadows chill and gray.
   And the land is dim with winter gloom,
Then for thee, my darling, love will have its way,
When the winds are moaning o'er the meadows chill and gray.

In the vernal dawning with the starting of the leaf,
   In the merry-chanting time of spring,
Love steals all my senses, oh, the happy-hearted thief!
In the vernal morning with the starting of the leaf.

Always, ever always, even in the autumn drear,
   When the days are sighing out their grief,
Thou art still my darling, dearest of the dear,
Always, ever always, even in the autumn drear.

SONG

60

My heart to thy heart,
　My hand to thine;
My lip to thy lips,
　Kisses are wine
Brewed for the lover in sunshine and shade;
Let me drink deep, then, my African maid.

Lily to lily,
　Rose unto rose;
My love to thy love
　Tenderly grows.
Rend not the oak and the ivy in twain,
Nor the swart maid from her swarthier swain.

A HYMN

Lead gently, Lord, and slow,
   For oh, my steps are weak,
And ever as I go,
   Some soothing sentence speak;

That I may turn my face
   Through doubt's obscurity
Toward thine abiding-place,
   E'en tho' I cannot see.

For lo, the way is dark;
   Through mist and cloud I grope,
Save for that fitful spark,
   The little flame of hope.

Lead gently, Lord, and slow,
   For fear that I may fall;
I know not where to go
   Unless I hear thy call.

My fainting soul doth yearn
   For thy green hills afar;
So let thy mercy burn—
   My greater, guiding star!

61

INSPIRATION

62

At the golden gate of song
Stood I, knocking all day long,
But the Angel, calm and cold,
Still refused and bade me, "Hold."

Then a breath of soft perfume,
Then a light within the gloom;
Thou, Love, camest to my side,
And the gates flew open wide.

Long I dwelt in this domain,
Knew no sorrow, grief, or pain;
Now you bid me forth and free,
Will you shut these gates on me?

A MUSICAL

Outside the rain upon the street,   63
   The sky all grim of hue,
Inside, the music-painful sweet,
   And yet I heard but you.

As is a thrilling violin,
   So is your voice to me,
And still above the other strains,
   It sang in ecstasy.

AND THAT
IS LIFE

LIFE

66

A crust of bread and a corner to sleep in,
A minute to smile and an hour to weep in,
A pint of joy to a peck of trouble,
And never a laugh but the moans come double;
    And that is life!

A crust and a corner that love makes precious,
With a smile to warm and the tears to refresh us;
And joy seems sweeter when cares come after,
And a moan is the finest of foils for laughter;
    And that is life!

THE SUM

A little dreaming by the way,
A little toiling day by day;
A little pain, a little strife,
A little joy,—and that is life.

A little short-lived summer's morn,
When joy seems all so newly born,
When one day's sky is blue above,
And one bird sings,—and that is love.

A little sickening of the years,
The tribute of a few hot tears,
Two folded hands, the failing breath,
And peace at last,—and that is death.

Just dreaming, loving, dying so,
The actors in the drama go—
A flitting picture on a wall,
Love, Death, the themes; but is that all?

UNEXPRESSED

68

Deep in my heart that aches with the repression,
  And strives with plenitude of bitter pain,
There lives a thought that clamors for expression,
  And spends its undelivered force in vain.

What boots it that some other may have thought it?
  The right of thoughts' expression is divine;
The price of pain I pay for it has bought it,
  I care not who lays claim to it—'t is mine!

And yet not mine until it be delivered;
  The manner of its birth shall prove the test.
Alas, alas, my rock of pride is shivered—
  I beat my brow—the thought still unexpressed.

MISAPPREHENSION

Out of my heart, one day, I wrote a song,
    With my heart's blood imbued,
Instinct with passion, tremulously strong,
    With grief subdued;
    Breathing a fortitude
        Pain-bought.
And one who claimed much love for what I wrought,
    Read and considered it,
        And spoke:
"Ay, brother,—'tis well writ,
    But where's the joke?"

THE CRISIS

A man of low degree was sore oppressed,
　　Fate held him under iron-handed sway,
And ever, those who saw him thus distressed
　　Would bid him bend his stubborn will and pray.
But he, strong in himself and obdurate,
Waged, prayerless, on his losing fight with Fate.

Friends gave his proferred hand their coldest clasp,
　　Or took it not at all; and Poverty,
That bruised his body with relentless grasp,
　　Grinned, taunting, when he struggled to be free.
But though with helpless hands he beat the air,
His need extreme yet found no voice in prayer.

Then he prevailed; and forthwith snobbish Fate,
　　Like some whipped cur, came fawning at his feet;
Those who had scorned forgave and called him great—
　　His friends found out that friendship still was sweet.
But he, once obdurate, now bowed his head
In prayer, and trembling with its import, said:

"Mere human strength may stand ill-fortune's frown;
　　So I prevailed, for human strength was mine;
But from the killing pow'r of great renown,
　　Naught may protect me save a strength divine.
Help me, O Lord, in this my trembling cause;
I scorn men's curses, but I dread applause!"

SYMPATHY

I know what the caged bird feels, alas!
   When the sun is bright on the upland slopes;
When the wind stirs soft through the springing grass,
And the river flows like a stream of glass;
   When the first bird sings and the first bud opes,
And the faint perfume from its chalice steals—
I know what the caged bird feels!

I know why the caged bird beats his wing
   Till its blood is red on the cruel bars;
For he must fly back to his perch and cling
When he fain would be on the bough a-swing;
   And a pain still throbs in the old, old scars
And they pulse again with a keener sting—
I know why he beats his wing!

I know why the caged bird sings, ah me,
   When his wing is bruised and his bosom sore,—
When he beats his bars and he would be free;
It is not a carol of joy or glee,
   But a prayer that he sends from his heart's deep core,
But a plea, that upward to Heaven he flings—
I know why the caged bird sings!

LIFE'S TRAGEDY

It may be misery not to sing at all
  And to go silent through the brimming day.
It may be sorrow never to be loved,
  But deeper griefs than these beset the way.

To have come near to sing the perfect song
  And only by a half-tone lost the key,
There is the potent sorrow, there the grief,
  The pale, sad staring of life's tragedy.

To have just missed the perfect love,
  Not the hot passion of untempered youth,
But that which lays aside its vanity
  And gives thee, for thy trusting worship, truth—

This, this it is to be accursed indeed;
  For if we mortals love, or if we sing,
We count our joys not by the things we have,
  But by what kept us from the perfect thing.

A PRAYER

O Lord, the hard-won miles   73
    Have worn my stumbling feet:
Oh, soothe me with thy smiles,
    And make my life complete.

The thorns were thick and keen
    Where'er I trembling trod;
The way was long between
    My wounded feet and God.

Where healing waters flow
    Do thou my footsteps lead.
My heart is aching so;
    Thy gracious balm I need.

THE GARRET

Within a London garret high,
Above the roofs and near the sky,
My ill-rewarding pen I ply
    To win me bread.
This little chamber, six by four,
Is castle, study, den, and more,—
Altho' no carpet decks the floor,
    Nor down, the bed.

My room is rather bleak and bare;
I only have one broken chair,
But then, there's plenty of fresh air,—
    Some light, beside.
What tho' I cannot ask my friends
To share with me my odds and ends,
A liberty my aerie lends,
    To most denied.

The bore who falters at the stair
No more shall be my curse and care,
And duns shall fail to find my lair
    With beastly bills.
When debts have grown and funds are short,
I find it rather pleasant sport
To live "above the common sort"
    With all their ills.

I write my rhymes and sing away,
And dawn may come or dusk or day:
Tho' fare be poor, my heart is gay,
    And full of glee.
Though chimney-pots be all my views;
'T is nearer for the winging Muse,
So I'm sure she'll not refuse
    To visit me.

SHIPS THAT PASS IN THE NIGHT

Out in the sky the great dark clouds are massing;
    I look far out into the pregnant night,
Where I can hear a solemn booming gun
    And catch the gleaming of a random light,
That tells me that the ship I seek is passing, passing.

My tearful eyes my soul's deep hurt are glassing;
    For I would hail and check that ship of ships.
I stretch my hands imploring, cry aloud,
    My voice falls dead a foot from mine own lips,
And but its ghost doth reach that vessel, passing, passing.

O Earth, O Sky, O Ocean, both surpassing,
    O heart of mine, O soul that dreads the dark!
Is there no hope for me? Is there no way
    That I may sight and check that speeding bark
Which out of sight and sound is passing, passing?

WE WEAR THE MASK

We wear the mask that grins and lies,
It hides our cheeks and shades our eyes,—
This debt we pay to human guile;
With torn and bleeding hearts we smile,
And mouth with myriad subtleties.

Why should the world be overwise,
In counting all our tears and sighs?
Nay, let them only see us, while
    We wear the mask.

We smile, but, O great Christ, our cries
To thee from tortured souls arise.
We sing, but oh the clap is vile
Beneath our feet, and long the mile;
But let the world dream otherwise,
    We wear the mask!

WHY FADES A DREAM

Why fades a dream?
   An iridescent ray
Flecked in between the tryst
   Of night and day.
   Why fades a dream?—
Of consciousness the shade
Wrought out by lack of light and made
   Upon life's stream.
   Why fades a dream?

That thought may thrive,
   So fades the fleshless dream;
Lest men should learn to trust
   The things that seem.
   So fades a dream,
That living thought may grow
And like a waxing star-beam glow
   Upon life's stream—
   So fades a dream.

THEOLOGY

78   There is a heaven, for ever, day by day,
The upward longing of my soul doth tell me so.
There is a hell, I'm quite as sure; for pray,
If there were not, where would my neighbours go?

THE BOHEMIAN

Bring me the livery of no other man.　　　　
　　I am my own to robe me at my pleasure.
　　Accepted rules to me disclose no treasure:
What is the chief who shall my garments plan?
　　No garb conventional but I'll attack it.
　　(Come, why not don my spangled jacket?)

DREAMS

Dream on, for dreams are sweet:
    Do not awaken!
Dream on, and at thy feet
    Pomegranates shall be shaken.

Who likeneth the youth
    Of life to morning?
'T is like the night in truth,
    Rose-coloured dreams adorning.

The wind is soft above,
    The shadows umber.
(There is a dream called Love.)
    Take thou the fullest slumber!

In Lethe's soothing stream,
    Thy thirst thou slakest.
Sleep, sleep; 't is sweet to dream.
    Oh, weep when thou awakest!

THE DREAMER

Temples he built and palaces of air,
   And, with the artist's parent-pride aglow,
   His fancy saw his vague ideals grow
Into creations marvellously fair;
He set his foot upon Fame's nether stair.
   But ah, his dream,—it had entranced him so
   He could not move. He could no farther go;
But passed in joy that he was even there!

He did not wake until one day there gleamed
   Thro' his dark consciousness a light that racked
His being till he rose, alert to act.
But lo! what he had dreamed, the while he dreamed,
   Another, wedding action unto thought,
   Into the living, pulsing world had brought.

COMPARISON

The sky of brightest gray seems dark
  To one whose sky was ever white.
To one who never knew a spark,
  Thro' all his life, of love or light,
  The grayest cloud seems over-bright.

The robin sounds a beggar's note
  Where one the nightingale has heard,
But he for whom no silver throat
  Its liquid music ever stirred,
  Deems robin still the sweetest bird.

THE MYSTERY

I was not; now I am—a few days hence
I shall not be; I fain would look before
And after, but can neither do; some Power
Or lack of power says "no" to all I would.
I stand upon a wide and sunless plain,
Nor chart nor steel to guide my steps aright.
Whene'er, o'ercoming fear, I dare to move,
I grope without direction and by chance.
Some feign to hear a voice and feel a hand
That draws them ever upward thro' the gloom.
But I —I hear no voice and touch no hand,
Tho' oft thro' silence infinite I list,
And strain my hearing to supernal sounds;
Tho' oft thro' fateful darkness do I reach,
And stretch my hand to find that other hand.
I question of th' eternal bending skies
That seem to neighbor with the novice earth;
But they roll on, and daily shut their eyes
On me, as I one day shall do on them,
And tell me not the secret that I ask.

VAGRANTS

Long time ago, we two set out,
 My soul and I.
 I know not why,
For all our way was dim with doubt.
 I know not where
 We two may fare:
Though still with every changing weather,
We wander, groping on together.

We do not love, we are not friends,
 My soul and I.
 He lives a lie;
Untruth lines every way he wends.
 A scoffer be
 Who jeers at me:
And so, my comrade and my brother,
We wander on and hate each other.

Ay, there be taverns and to spare,
 Beside the road;
 But some strange goad
Lets me not stop to taste their fare.
 Knew I the goal
 Toward which my soul
And I made way, hope made life fragrant:
But no. We wander, aimless, vagrant!

THE REAL QUESTION

Folks is talkin' 'bout de money, 'bout de silvah an' de gold;
All de time de season's changin' and' de days is gittin' cold.
An' dey's wond'rin' 'bout de metals, whethah we'll have one er
    two,
While de price o' coal is risin' an' dey's two months' rent dat's
    due.

Some folks says dat gold's de only money dat is wuff de name,
Den de othahs rise an' tell 'em dat dey ought to be ashame,
An' dat silvah is de only thing to save us f'om de powah
Of de gold-bug ragin' 'roun' an seekin' who he may devowah.

Well, you folks kin keep on shoutin' wif yo' gold er silvah cry,
But I tell you people hams is sceerce an' fowls is roostin' high.
An' hit ain't de so't o' money dat is pesterin' my min',
But de question I want answehed's how to get at any kin'!

DREAMS

What dreams we have and how they fly
Like rosy clouds across the sky;
   Of wealth, of fame, of sure success,
   Of love that comes to cheer and bless;
And how they wither, how they fade,
The waning wealth, the jilting jade—
   The fame that for a moment gleams.
   Then flies forever,—dreams, ah—dreams!

O burning doubt and long regret,
O tears with which our eyes are wet,
   Heart-throbs, heart-aches, the glut of pain,
   The somber cloud, the bitter rain,
You were not of those dreams—ah! well,
Your full fruition who can tell?
   Wealth, fame, and love, ah! love that beams
   Upon our souls, all dreams—ah! dreams.

HYMN

When storms arise
And dark'ning skies
   About me threat'ning lower,
To thee, O Lord, I raise mine eyes,
To thee my tortured spirit flies
   For solace in that hour.

The mighty arm
Will let no harm
   Come near me nor befall me;
Thy voice shall quiet my alarm,
When life's great battle waxeth warm—
   No foeman shall appall me.

Upon thy breast
Secure I rest,
   From sorrow and vexation;
No more by sinful cares oppressed,
But in thy presence ever blest,
   O God of my salvation.

RELIGION

I am no priest of crooks nor creeds,
For human wants and human needs
Are more to me than prophets' deeds;
And human tears and human cares
Affect me more than human prayers.

Go, cease your wail, lugubrious saint!
You fret high Heaven with your plaint.
Is this the "Christian's joy" you paint?
Is this the Christian's boasted bliss?
Avails your faith no more than this?

Take up your arms, come out with me,
Let Heav'n alone; humanity
Needs more and Heaven less from thee.
With pity for mankind look 'round;
Help them to rise—and Heaven is found.

CONSCIENCE AND REMORSE

"Good-bye," I said to my conscience—
   "Good-bye for aye and aye,"
And I put her hands off harshly,
   And turned my face away;
And conscience smitten sorely
   Returned not from that day.

But a time came when my spirit
   Grew weary of its pace;
And I cried: "Come back, my conscience;
   I long to see thy face."
But conscience cried "I cannot;
   Remorse sits in my place."

Slow moves the pageant of a climbing race;
   Their footsteps drag far, far below the height,
   And, unprevailing by their utmost might,
Seem faltering downward from each hard won place.
No strange, swift-sprung exception we; we trace
   A devious way thro' dim, uncertain light,—
   Our hope, through the long vistaed years, a sight
Of that our Captain's soul sees face to face.
   Who, faithless, faltering that the road is steep,
Now raiseth up his drear insistent cry?
   Who stoppeth here to spend a while in sleep
Or curseth that the storm obscures the sky?
   Heed not the darkness round you, dull and deep;
The clouds grow thickest when the summit's nigh.

THE DEBT

This is the debt I pay
Just for one riotous day,
Years of regret and grief,
Sorrow without relief.

Pay it I will to the end—
Until the grave, my friend,
Gives me a true release—
Gives me the clasp of peace.

Slight was the thing I bought,
Small was the debt I thought,
Poor was the loan at best—
God! but the interest!

He had his dream, and all through life,
Worked up to it through toil and strife.
Afloat fore'er before his eyes,
It colored for him all his skies:
    The storm-cloud dark
    Above his bark,
The calm and listless vault of blue
Took on his hopeful hue,
It tinctured every passing beam—
    He had his dream.

He labored hard and failed at last,
His sails too weak to bear the blast,
The raging tempests tore away
And sent his beating bark astray.
    But what cared he
    For wind or sea!
He said, "The tempest will be short,
My bark will come to port."
He saw through every cloud a gleam—
    He had his dream.

WITH THE LARK

Night is for sorrow and dawn is for joy,
Chasing the troubles that fret and annoy;
Darkness for sighing and daylight for song,—
Cheery and chaste the strain, heartfelt and strong.
All the night through, though I moan in the dark,
I wake in the morning to sing with the lark.

Deep in the midnight the rain whips the leaves,
Softly and sadly the wood-spirit grieves.
But when the first hue of dawn tints the sky,
I shall shake out my wings like the birds and be dry;
And though, like the rain-drops, I grieved through the dark,
I shall wake in the morning to sing with the lark.

On the high hills of heaven, some morning to be,
Where the rain shall not grieve thro' the leaves of the tree,
There my heart will be glad for the pain I have known,
For my hand will be clasped in the hand of mine own;
And though life has been hard and death's pathway been dark,
I shall wake in the morning to sing with the lark.

By rugged ways and thro' the night
We struggle blindly toward the light;
And groping, stumbling, ever pray
For sight of long delaying day.
The cruel thorns beside the road
Stretch eager points our steps to goad,
And from the thickets all about
Detaining hands reach threatening out.

94

"Deliver us, oh, Lord," we cry,
Our hands uplifted to the sky.
No answer save the thunder's peal,
And onward, onward, still we reel.
"Oh, give us now thy guiding light";
Our sole reply, the lightning's blight.
"Vain, vain," cries one, "in vain we call";
But faith serene is over all.

Beside our way the streams are dried,
And famine mates us side by side.
Discouraged and reproachful eyes
Seek once again the frowning skies.
Yet shall there come, spite storm and shock,
A Moses who shall smite the rock,
Call manna from the Giver's hand,
And lead us to the promised land!

The way is dark and cold and steep,
And shapes of horror murder sleep,
And hard the unrelenting years;
But 'twixt our sighs and moans and tears,
We still can smile, we still can sing,
Despite the arduous journeying.
For faith and hope their courage lend,
And rest and light are at the end.

AT SUNSET TIME

Adown the west a golden glow
    Sinks burning in the sea,
And all the dreams of long ago
    Come flooding back to me.
The past has writ a story strange
    Upon my aching heart,
But time has wrought a subtle change,
    My wounds have ceased to smart.

No more the quick delight of youth,
    No more the sudden pain,
I look no more for trust or truth
    Where greed may compass gain.
What, was it I who bared my heart
    Through unrelenting years,
And knew the sting of misery's dart,
    The tang of sorrow's tears?

'Tis better now, I do not weep,
    I do not laugh nor care;
My soul and spirit half asleep
    Drift aimless everywhere.
We float upon a sluggish stream,
    We ride no rapids mad,
While life is all a tempered dream
    And every joy half sad.

BEYOND
THE YEARS

BEYOND THE YEARS

I

Beyond the years the answer lies,
Beyond where brood the grieving skies
        And Night drops tears.
Where Faith rod-chastened smiles to rise
        And doff its fears,
And carping Sorrow pines and dies—
        Beyond the years.

II

Beyond the years the prayer for rest
Shall beat no more within the breast;
        The darkness clears,
And Morn perched on the mountain's crest
        Her form uprears—
The day that is to come is best,
        Beyond the years.

III

Beyond the years the soul shall find
That endless peace for which it pined,
        For light appears,
And to the eyes that still were blind
        With blood and tears,
Their sight shall come all unconfined
        Beyond the years.

FOREVER

I had not known before
    Forever was so long a word.
The slow stroke of the clock of time
    I had not heard.

'Tis hard to learn so late;
    It seems no sad heart really learns,
But hopes and trusts and doubts and fears,
    And bleeds and burns.

The night is not all dark,
    Nor is the day all it seems,
But each may bring me this relief—
    My dreams and dreams.

I had not known before
    That Never was so sad a word,
So wrap me in forgetfulness—
    I have not heard.

BEHIND THE ARRAS

As in some dim baronial hall restrained,
A prisoner sits, engirt by secret doors
And waving tapestries that argue forth
Strange passages into the outer air;
So in this dimmer room which we call life,
Thus sits the soul and marks with eye intent
That mystic curtain o'er the portal death;
Still deeming that behind the arras lies
The lambent way that leads to lasting light.
Poor fooled and foolish soul! Know now that death
Is but a blind, false door that nowhere leads,
And gives no hope of exit final, free.

MORTALITY

Ashes to ashes, dust unto dust,
What of his loving, what of his lust?
What of his passion, what of his pain?
What of his poverty, what of his pride?
Earth, the great mother, has called him again:
Deeply he sleeps, the world's verdict defied.
Shall he be tried again? Shall he go free?
Who shall the court convene? Where shall it be?
No answer on the land, none from the sea.
Only we know that as he did, we must:
You with your theories, you with your trust,—
Ashes to ashes, dust to dust!

WHEN ALL IS DONE

When all is done, and my last word is said,
And ye who loved me murmur, "He is dead,"
Let no one weep, for fear that I should know,
And sorrow too that ye should sorrow so.

When all is done and in the oozing clay,
Ye lay this cast-off hull of mine away,
Pray not for me, for, after long despair,
The quiet of the grave will be a prayer.

For I have suffered loss and grievous pain,
The hurts of hatred and the world's disdain,
And wounds so deep that love, well-tried and pure,
Had not the pow'r to ease them or to cure.

When all is done, say not my day is o'er,
And that thro' night I seek a dimmer shore:
Say rather that my morn has just begun,—
I greet the dawn and not a setting sun,
When all is done.

A DEATH SONG

Lay me down beneaf de willers in de grass,
Whah de branch'll go a-singin' as it pass.
 An' w'en I's a-layin' low,
 I kin hyeah it as it go
Singin', "Sleep, my honey, tek yo' res' at las'."

Lay me nigh to whah hit meks a little pool,
An' de watah stan's so quiet lak an' cool,
 Whah de little birds in spring,
 Ust to come an' drink an' sing,
An' de chillen waded on dey way to school.

Let me settle w'en my shouldahs draps dey load
Nigh enough to hyeah de noises in de road,
 Fu' I t'ink de las' long res'
 Gwine to soothe my sperrit bes'
Ef I's layin' 'mong de t'ings I's allus knowed.

TO A DEAD FRIEND

It is as if a silver chord
  Were suddenly grown mute,
And life's song with its rhythm warred
  Against a silver lute.

It is as if a silence fell
  Where bides the garnered sheaf,
And voices murmuring, "It is well,"
  Are stifled by our grief.

It is as if the gloom of night
  Had hid a summer's day,
And willows, sighing at their plight,
  Bent low beside the way.

For he was part of all the best
  That Nature loves and gives,
And ever more on Memory's breast
  He lies and laughs and lives.

THE MASTERS

Oh, who is the Lord of the land of life,
    When hotly goes the fray?
When, fierce we smile in the midst of strife
    Then whom shall we obey?

Oh, Love is the Lord of the land of life
    Who holds a monarch's sway;
He wends with wish of maid and wife,
    And him you must obey.

Then who is the Lord of the land of life,
    At setting of the sun?
Whose word shall sway when Peace is rife
    And all the fray is done?

Then Death is the Lord of the land of life,
    When your hot race is run.
Meet then his scythe and pruning-knife
    When the fray is lost or won.

THE MYSTIC SEA

106

The smell of the sea in my nostrils,
    The sound of the sea in mine ears;
The touch of the spray on my burning face,
    Like the mist of reluctant tears.

The blue of the sky above me,
    The green of the waves beneath;
The sun flashing down on a gray-white sail
    Like a scimitar from its sheath.

And ever the breaking billows,
    And ever the rocks' disdain;
And ever a thrill in mine inmost heart
    That my reason cannot explain.

So I say to my heart, "Be silent,
    The mystery of time is here;
Death's way will be plain when we fathom the main,
    And the secret of life be clear."

DEAD

A knock is at her door, but she is weak;
Strange dews have washed the paint streaks from her cheek;
She does not rise, but, ah, this friend is known,
And knows that he will find her all alone.
So opens he the door, and with soft tread
Goes straightaway to the richly curtained bed.
His soft hand on her dewy head he lays.
A strange white light she gives him for his gaze.
Then, looking on the glory of her charms,
He crushes her resistless in his arms.

Stand back! look not upon this bold embrace,
Nor view the calmness of the wanton's face;
With joy unspeakable and 'bated breath,
She keeps her last, long liaison with death!

COMPENSATION

Because I had loved so deeply,
   Because I had loved so long,
God in His great compassion
   Gave me the gift of song.

Because I have loved so vainly,
   And sung with such faltering breath,
The Master in infinite mercy
   Offers the boon of Death.

DESPAIR

Let me close the eyes of my soul
   That I may not see
What stands between thee and me.

Let me shut the ears of my heart
   That I may not hear
A voice that drowns yours, my dear.

Let me cut the cords of my life,
   Of my desolate being,
Since cursed is my hearing and seeing.

ERE SLEEP COMES DOWN TO SOOTHE
THE WEARY EYES

Ere sleep comes down to soothe the weary eyes,
    Which all the day with ceaseless care have sought
The magic gold which from the seeker flies;
    Ere dreams put on the gown and cap of thought,
And make the waking world a world of lies,—
    Of lies most palpable, uncouth, forlorn,
That say life's full of aches and tears and sighs,—
    Oh, how with more than dreams the soul is torn,
Ere sleep comes down to soothe the weary eyes.

Ere sleep comes down to soothe the weary eyes,
    How all the griefs and heartaches we have known
Come up like pois'nous vapors that arise
    From some base witch's caldron, when the crone,
To work some potent spell, her magic plies.
    The past which held its share of bitter pain,
Whose ghost we prayed that Time might exorcise,
    Comes up, is lived and suffered o'er again,
Ere sleep comes down to soothe the weary eyes.

Ere sleep comes down to soothe the weary eyes,
    What phantoms fill the dimly lighted room;
What ghostly shades in awe-creating guise
    Are bodied forth within the teeming gloom.
What echoes faint of sad and soul-sick cries,
    And pangs of vague inexplicable pain
That pay the spirit's ceaseless enterprise,
    Come thronging through the chambers of the brain,
Ere sleep comes down to soothe the weary eyes.

Ere sleep comes down to soothe the weary eyes,
    Where ranges forth the spirit far and free?
Through what strange realms and unfamiliar skies
    Tends her far course to lands of mystery?
To lands unspeakable—beyond surmise,
    Where shapes unknowable to being spring,
Till, faint of wing, the Fancy fails and dies
    Much wearied with the spirit's journeying,
Ere sleep comes down to soothe the weary eyes.

Ere sleep comes down to soothe the weary eyes,
    How questioneth the soul that other soul,—
The inner sense which neither cheats nor lies,
    But self exposes unto self, a scroll
Full writ with all life's acts unwise or wise,
    In characters indelible and known;
So, trembling with the shock of sad surprise,
    The soul doth view its awful self alone,
Ere sleep comes down to soothe the weary eyes.

When sleep comes down to seal the weary eyes,
    The last dear sleep whose soft embrace is balm,
And whom sad sorrow teaches us to prize
    For kissing all our passions into calm,
Ah, then, no more we heed the sad world's cries,
    Or seek to probe th' eternal mystery,
Or fret our souls at long-withheld replies,
    At glooms through which our visions cannot see,
When sleep comes down to seal the weary eyes.

THE PARADOX

I am the mother of sorrows,
    I am the ender of grief;
I am the bud and the blossom,
    I am the late-falling leaf.

I am thy priest and thy poet,
    I am thy serf and thy king;
I cure the tears of the heartsick,
    When I come near they shall sing.

White are my hands as the snowdrop;
    Swart are my fingers as clay;
Dark is my frown as the midnight,
    Fair is my brow as the day.

Battle and war are my minions,
    Doing my will as divine;
I am the calmer of passions,
    Peace is a nursling of mine.

Speak to me gently or curse me,
    Seek me or fly from my sight;
I am thy fool in the morning,
    Thou art my slave in the night.

Down to the grave will I take thee,
    Out from the noise of the strife;
Then shalt thou see me and know me—
    Death, then, no longer, but life.

Then shalt thou sing at my coming,
  Kiss me with passionate breath,
Clasp me and smile to have thought me
  Aught save the foeman of Death.

Come to me, brother, when weary,
  Come when thy lonely heart swells;
I'll guide thy footsteps and lead thee
  Down where the Dream Woman dwells.

PREMONITION

Dear heart, good-night!
Nay, list awhile that sweet voice singing
    When the world is all so bright,
And the sound of song set the heart a-ringing,
    Oh, love, it is not right—
    Not then to say, "Good-night."

Dear heart, good-night!
The late winds in the lake weeds shiver,
    And the spray flies cold and white.
And the voice that sings gives a telltale quiver—
    "Ah, yes, the world is bright,
    But, dearest heart, good-night!"

Dear heart, good-night!
And do not longer seek to hold me!
    For my soul is in affright
As the fearful glooms in their pall enfold me.
    See him who sang how white
    And still; so, dear, good-night.

Dear heart, good-night!
Thy hand I'll press no more forever,
    And mine eyes shall lose the light;
For the great white wraith by the winding river
    Shall check my steps with might.
    So, dear, good-night, good-night!

THE FOREST GREETING

Good hunting!—aye, good hunting,
    Wherever the forest call;
But ever a heart beats hot with fear,
    And what of the birds that fall?

Good hunting!—aye, good hunting,
    Wherever the north winds blow;
But what of the stag that calls for his mate?
    And what of the wounded doe?

Good hunting!—aye, good hunting;
    And ah! we are bold and strong;
But our triumph call through the forest hall
    Is a brother's funeral song.

For we are brothers ever,
    Panther and bird and bear;
Man and the weakest that fear his face,
    Born to the nest or lair.

Yes, brothers, and who shall judge us?
    Hunters and game are we;
But who gave the right for me to smite?
    Who boasts when he smiteth me?

Good hunting!—aye, good hunting,
    And dim is the forest track;
But the sportsman Death comes striding on:
    Brothers, the way is black.

Pray why are you so bare, so bare,
   Oh, bough of the old oak-tree;
And why, when I go through the shade you throw,
   Runs a shudder over me?

My leaves were green as the best, I trow,
   And sap ran free in my veins,
But I saw in the moonlight dim and weird
   A guiltless victim's pains.

I bent me down to hear his sigh;
   I shook with his gurgling moan,
And I trembled sore when they rode away,
   And left him here alone.

They'd charged him with the old, old crime,
   And set him fast in jail:
Oh, why does the dog howl all night long,
   And why does the night wind wail?

He prayed his prayer and he swore his oath,
   And he raised his hand to the sky;
But the beat of hoofs smote on his ear,
   And the steady tread drew nigh.

Who is it rides by night, by night,
   Over the moonlit road?
And what is the spur that keeps the pace,
   What is the galling goad?

And now they beat at the prison door,
   "Ho, keeper, do not stay!
We are friends of him whom you hold within,
   And we fain would take him away

"From those who ride fast on our heels
    With mind to do him wrong;
They have no care for his innocence,
    And the rope they bear is long."

They have fooled the jailer with lying words,
    They have fooled the man with lies;
The bolts unbar, the locks are drawn,
    And the great door open flies.

Now they have taken him from the jail,
    And hard and fast they ride,
And the leader laughs low down in his throat,
    As they halt my trunk beside.

Oh, the judge, he wore a mask of black,
    And the doctor one of white,
And the minister, with his oldest son,
    Was curiously bedight.

Oh, foolish man, why weep you now?
    'T is but a little space,
And the time will come when these shall dread
    The mem'ry of your face.

I feel the rope against my bark,
    And the weight of him in my grain,
I feel in the throe of his final woe
    The touch of my own last pain.

And never more shall leaves come forth
   On a bough that bears the ban;
I am burned with dread, I am dried and dead,
   From the curse of a guiltless man.

And ever the judge rides by, rides by,
   And goes to hunt the deer,
And ever another rides his soul
   In the guise of a mortal fear.

And ever the man he rides me hard,
   And never a night stays he;
For I feel his curse as a haunted bough,
   On the trunk of a haunted tree.

DEATH

Storm and strife and stress,
Lost in a wilderness,
Groping to find a way,
Forth to the haunts of day.

Sudden a vista peeps,
Out of the tangled deeps,
Only a point—the ray
But at the end is day.

THE MAJESTY
OF GOD

NIGHT

Silence, and whirling worlds afar
   Through all encircling skies.
What floods come o'er the spirit's bar,
   What wondrous thoughts arise.

The earth, a mantle falls away,
   And, winged, we leave the sod;
Where shines in its eternal sway
   The majesty of God.

PREPARATION

The little bird sits in the nest and sings
   A shy, soft song to the morning light;
And it flutters a little and prunes its wings.
   The song is halting and poor and brief,
   And the fluttering wings scarce stir a leaf;
But the note is a prelude to sweeter things,
And the busy bill and the flutter slight
Are proving the wings for a bolder flight!

A DROWSY DAY

The air is dark, the sky is gray,
    The misty shadows come and go,
And here within my dusky room
Each chair looks ghostly in the gloom.
    Outside the rain falls cold and slow—
Half-stinging drops, half-blinding spray.

Each slightest sound is magnified,
    For drowsy quiet holds her reign;
The burnt stick in the fireplace breaks,
The nodding cat with start awakes,
    And then to sleep drops off again,
Unheeding Towser at her side.

I look far out across the lawn,
    Where huddled stand the silly sheep;
My work lies idle at my hands,
My thoughts fly out like scattered strands
    Of thread, and on the verge of sleep—
Still half awake—I dream and yawn.

What spirits rise before my eyes!
    How various of kind and form!
Sweet memories of days long past,
The dreams of youth that could not last,
    Each smiling calm, each raging storm,
That swept across my early skies.

Half seen, the bare, gaunt-fingered boughs
    Before my window sweep and sway,
And chafe in tortures of unrest.
My chin sinks down upon my breast;
    I cannot work on such a day,
But only sit and dream and drowse.

THE SPARROW

A little bird, with plumage brown,
Beside my window flutters down,
A moment chirps its little strain,
Then taps upon my window-pane,
And chirps again, and hops along,
To call my notice to its song;
But I work on, nor heed its lay,
Till, in neglect, it flies away.

So birds of peace and hope and love
Come fluttering earthward from above,
To settle on life's window-sills,
And ease our load of earthly ills;
But we, in traffic's rush and din
Too deep engaged to let them in,
With deadened heart and sense plod on,
Nor know our loss till they are gone.

A SUMMER'S NIGHT

The night is dewy as a maiden's mouth,
   The skies are bright as are a maiden's eyes,
   Soft as a maiden's breath the wind that flies
Up from the perfumed bosom of the South.
Like sentinels, the pines stand in the park;
   And hither hastening, like rakes that roam,
   With lamps to light their wayward footsteps home,
The fireflies come stagg'ring down the dark.

SPRING SONG

A blue-bell springs upon the ledge,
A lark sits singing in the hedge;
Sweet perfumes scent the balmy air,
And life is brimming everywhere.
What lark and breeze and bluebird sing,
     Is Spring, Spring, Spring!

No more the air is sharp and cold;
The planter wends across the wold,
And, glad, beneath the shining sky
We wander forth, my love and I.
And ever in our hearts doth ring
     This song of Spring, Spring!

For life is life and love is love,
'Twixt maid and man or dove and dove.
Life may be short, life may be long,
But love will come, and to its song
Shall this refrain for ever cling
     Of Spring, Spring, Spring!

CHANGING TIME

The cloud looked in at the window,
   And said to the day, "Be dark!"
And the roguish rain tapped hard on the pane,
   To stifle the song of the lark.

The wind sprang up in the tree tops
   And shrieked with a voice of death,
But the rough-voiced breeze, that shook the trees,
   Was touched with a violet's breath.

SUNSET

The river sleeps beneath the sky,
   And clasps the shadows to its breast;
The crescent moon shines dim on high;
   And in the lately radiant west
      The gold is fading into gray.
      Now stills the lark his festive lay,
      And mourns with me the dying day.

While in the south the first faint star
   Lifts to the night its silver face,
And twinkles to the moon afar
   Across the heaven's graying space,
Low murmurs reach me from the town,
As Day puts on her sombre crown,
And shakes her mantel darkly down.

DAWN

An angel, robed in spotless white,
Bent down and kissed the sleeping Night.
Night woke to blush; the sprite was gone.
Men saw the blush and called it Dawn.

RAIN-SONGS

The rain streams down like harp-strings from the sky;
    The wind, that world-old harpist sitteth by;
And ever as he sings his low refrain,
    He plays upon the harp-strings of the rain.

ROSES

Oh, wind of the spring-time, oh, free wind of May,
  When blossoms and bird-song are rife;
Oh, joy for the season, and joy for the day,
  That gave me the roses of life, of life,
  That gave me the roses of life.

Oh, wind of the summer, sing loud in the night,
  When flutters my heart like a dove;
One came from thy kingdom, thy realm of delight,
  And gave me the roses of love, of love,
  And gave me the roses of love.

Oh, wind of the winter, sigh low in thy grief,
  I hear thy compassionate breath;
I wither, I fall, like the autumn-kissed leaf,
  He gave me the roses of death, of death,
  He gave me the roses of death.

MORNING

The mist has left the greening plain,
The dew-drops shine like fairy rain,
The coquette rose awakes again
   Her lovely self adorning.
The Wind is hiding in the trees,
A sighing, soothing, laughing tease,
Until the rose says "Kiss me, please,"
   'Tis morning, 'tis morning.

With staff in hand and careless-free,
The wanderer fares right jauntily,
For towns and houses are, thinks he,
   For scorning, for scorning.
My soul is swift upon the wing,
And in its deeps a song I bring;
Come, Love, and we together sing,
   " 'Tis morning, 'tis morning."

BY THE STREAM

134   By the stream I dream in calm delight, and watch as in a glass,
How the clouds like crowds of snowy-hued and white-robed
     maidens pass,
And the water into ripples breaks and sparkles as it spreads,
Like a host of armored knights with silver helmets on their heads.
And I deem the stream an emblem fit of human life may go,
For I find a mind may sparkle much and yet but shallows show,
And a soul may glow with myriad lights and wondrous mysteries,
When it only lies a dormant thing and mirrors what it sees.

SILENCE

'T is better to sit here beside the sea,   135
    Here on the spray-kissed beach,
In silence, that between such friends as we
    Is full of deepest speech.

A WINTER'S DAY

Across the hills and down the narrow ways,
   And up the valley where the free winds sweep,
   The earth is folded in an ermined sleep
That mocks the melting mirth of myriad Mays.
Departed her disheartening duns and grays,
   And all her crusty black is covered deep.
   Dark streams are locked in Winter's donjon-keep,
And made to shine with keen, unwonted rays.
O icy mantle, and deceitful snow!
   What world-old liars in your hearts ye are!
   Are there not still the darkened seam and scar
Beneath the brightness that you fain would show?
Come from the cover with thy blot and blur,
O reeking Earth, thou whited sepulchre!

TO A VIOLET FOUND ON ALL SAINT'S DAY

Belated wanderer of the ways of spring,
    Lost in the chill of grim November rain,
Would I could read the message that you bring
    And find in it the antidote for pain.

Does some sad spirit out beyond the day,
    Far looking to the hours forever dead,
Send you a tender offering to lay
    Upon the grave of us, the living dead?

Or does some brighter spirit, unforlorn,
    Send you, my little sister of the wood,
To say to some one on a cloudful born,
    "Life lives through death, my brother, all is good"?

With meditative hearts the others go
    The memory of their dead to dress anew.
But, sister mine, bide here that I may know,
    Life grows, through death, as beautiful as you.

OCTOBER

October is the treasurer of the year,
    And all the months pay bounty to her store;
The fields and orchards still their tribute bear,
    And fill her brimming coffers more and more.
But she, with youthful lavishness,
Spends all her wealth in gaudy dress,
    And decks herself in garments bold
    Of scarlet, purple, red, and gold.

She heedeth not how swift the hours fly,
    But smiles and sings her happy life along;
She only sees above a shining sky;
    She only hears the breezes' voice in song.
Her garments trail the woodlands through,
And gather pearls of early dew
    That sparkle, till the roguish Sun
    Creeps up and steals them every one.

But what cares she that jewels should be lost,
    When all of Nature's bounteous wealth is hers?
Though princely fortunes may have been their cost,
    Not one regret her calm demeanor stirs.
Whole-hearted, happy, careless, free,
She lives her life out joyously,
    Nor cares when Frost stalks o'er her way
    And turns her auburn locks to gray.

A LAZY DAY

The trees bend down along the stream,
    Where anchored swings my tiny boat.
The day is one to drowse and dream
    And list the thrush's throttling note.
When music from his bosom bleeds
Among the river's rustling reeds.

No ripple stirs the placid pool,
    When my adventurous line is cast,
A truce to sport, while clear and cool,
    The mirrored clouds slide softly past.
The sky gives back a blue divine,
And all the world's wide wealth is mine.

A pickerel leaps, a bow of light,
The minnows shine from side to side.
The first faint breeze comes up the tide—
I pause with half uplifted oar,
While night drifts down to claim the shore.

GIVE US
COMFORT

DOUGLASS

Ah, Douglass, we have fall'n on evil days,
    Such days as thou, not even thou didst know,
    When thee, the eyes of that harsh long ago
Saw, salient, at the cross of devious ways,
And all the country heard thee with amaze.
    Not ended then, the passionate ebb and flow,
    The awful tide that battled to and fro;
We ride amid a tempest of dispraise.

Now, when the waves of swift dissension swarm,
    And Honor, the strong pilot, lieth stark,
Oh, for thy voice high-sounding o'er the storm,
    For thy strong arm to guide the shivering bark,
The blast-defying power of thy form,
    To give us comfort through the lonely dark.

BOOKER T. WASHINGTON

The word is writ that he who runs may read.
What is the passing breath of earthly fame?
But to snatch glory from the hands of blame—
That is to be, to live, to strive indeed.
A poor Virginia cabin gave the seed,
And from its dark and lowly door there came
A peer of princes in the world's acclaim,
A master spirit for the nation's need.
Strong, silent, purposeful beyond his kind,
    The mark of rugged force on brow and lip,
Straight on he goes, nor turns to look behind
    Where hot the hounds come baying at his hip;
With one idea foremost in his mind,
    Like the keen prow of some on-forging ship.

LINCOLN

144

Hurt was the nation with a mighty wound,
And all her ways were filled with clam'rous sound.
Wailed loud the South with unremitting grief,
And wept the North that could not find relief.
Then madness joined its harshest tone to strife:
A minor note swelled in the song of life.
Till, stirring with the love that filled his breast,
But still, unflinching at the right's behest,
Grave Lincoln came, strong handed, from afar,
The mighty Homer of the lyre of war.
'T was he who bade the raging tempest cease,
Wrenched from his harp the harmony of peace,
Muted the strings, that made the discord,—Wrong,
And gave his spirit up in thund'rous song.
Oh mighty Master of the mighty lyre,
Earth heard and trembled at thy strains of fire,
Earth learned of thee what Heav'n already knew,
And wrote thee down among her treasured few.

HARRIET BEECHER STOWE

She told the story, and the whole world wept
   At wrongs and cruelties it had not known
   But for this fearless woman's voice alone.
   She spoke to consciences that long had slept:
Her message, Freedom's clear reveille, swept
   From heedless hovel to complacent throne.
   Command and prophecy were in the tone
   And from its sheath the sword of justice leapt.
Around two peoples swelled a fiery wave,
   But both came forth transfigured from the flame.
Blest be the hand that dared be strong to save,
   And blest be she who in our weakness came—
Prophet and priestess! At one stroke she gave
   A race to freedom and herself to fame.

146

Why was it that the thunder voice of Fate
    Should call thee, studious, from the classic groves,
    Where calm-eyed Pallas with still footstep roves,
And charge thee seek the turmoil of the state?
What bade thee hear the voice and rise elate,
    Leave home and kindred and thy spicy loaves,
    To lead th' unlettered and despised droves
To manhood's home and thunder at the gate?

Far better the slow blaze of Learning's light,
    The cool and quiet of her dearer fane,
Than this hot terror of a hopeless fight,
    This cold endurance of the final pain,—
Since thou and those who with thee died for right
    Have died, the Present teaches, but in vain!

ALEXANDER CRUMMELL—DEAD

Back to the breast of thy mother,
Child of the earth!
E'en her caress can not smother
What thou hast done.
Follow the trail of the westering sun
Over the earth.
Thy light and his were as one—
Sun, in thy worth.
Unto a nation whose sky was as night,
Camest thou, holily, bearing thy light:
And the dawn came,
In it thy fame
Flashed up in a flame.

Back to the breast of thy mother—
To rest.
Long hast thou striven;
Dared where the hills by the lightning of heaven were riven;
Go now, pure shriven.
Who shall come after thee, out of the clay—
Learned one and leader to show us the way?
Who shall rise up when the world gives the test?
Think thou no more of this—
Rest!

I SING
MY SONG

A song is but a little thing,
And yet what joy it is to sing!
In hours of toil it gives me zest,
And when at eve I long for rest;
When cows come home along the bars,
    And in the fold I hear the bell,
As Night, the shepherd, herds his stars,
    I sing my song, and all is well.

There are no ears to hear my lays,
No lips to lift a word of praise;
But still, with faith unfaltering,
I live and laugh and love and sing.
What matters yon unheeding throng?
    They cannot feel my spirit's spell,
Since life is sweet and love is long,
    I sing my song, and all is well.

My days are never days of ease;
I till my ground and prune my trees.
When ripened gold is all the plain,
I put my sickle to the grain.
I labor hard, and toil and sweat,
    While others dream within the dell;
But even while my brow is wet,
    I sing my song, and all is well.

Sometimes the sun, unkindly hot,
My garden makes a desert spot;
Sometimes a blight upon the tree
Takes all my fruit away from me;
And then with throes of bitter pain
    Rebellious passions rise and swell;
But—life is more than fruit or grain,
    And so I sing, and all is well.

A SAILOR'S SONG

Oh for the breath of the briny deep,
And the tug of the bellying sail,
With the sea-gull's cry across the sky
And a passing boatman's hail.
For, be she fierce or be she gay,
The sea is a famous friend alway.

Ho! for the plains where the dolphins play,
And the bend of the mast and spars,
And a fight at night with the wild sea-sprite
When the foam has drowned the stars.
And, pray, what joy can the landsman feel
Like the rise and fall of a sliding keel?

Fair is the mead; the lawn is fair
And the birds sing sweet on the lea;
But the echo soft of a song aloft
Is the strain that pleases me;
And swish of rope and ring of chain
Are music to men who sail the main.

Then, if you love me, let me sail
While a vessel dares the deep;
For the ship's my wife, and the breath of life
Are the raging gales that sweep;
And when I'm done with calm and blast,
A slide o'er the side, and rest at last.

THE FARM CHILD'S LULLABY

Oh, the little bird is rocking in the cradle of the wind,
   And it's bye, my little wee one, bye;
The harvest all is gathered and the pippins all are binned;
   Bye, my little wee one, bye;
The little rabbit's hiding in the golden shock of corn,
The thrifty squirrel's laughing bunny's idleness to scorn;
You are smiling with the angels in your slumber, smile till morn;
   So it's bye, my little wee one, bye.

There'll be plenty in the cellar, there'll be plenty on the shelf;
   Bye, my little wee one, bye;
There'll be goodly store of sweetings for a dainty little elf;
   Bye, my little one, bye.
The snow may be a-flying o'er the meadow and the hill,
The ice has checked the chatter of the little laughing rill,
But in your cosy cradle you are warm and happy still;
   So bye, my little wee one, bye.

Why, the Bob White thinks, the snowflake is a brother to his
     song;
   Bye, my little wee one, bye;
And the chimney sings the sweeter when the wind is blowing
     strong;
   Bye, my little wee one, bye;
The granary's overflowing, full is cellar, crib, and bin,
The wood has paid its tribute and the ax has ceased its din;
The winter may not harm you when you're sheltered safe within;
   So bye, my little wee one, bye.

THE FISHER CHILD'S LULLABY

The wind is out in its rage to-night,
   And your father is far at sea.
The rime on the window is hard and white
   But dear, you are near to me.
     Heave ho, weave low,
       Waves of the briny deep;
     Seethe low and breathe low,
       But sleep you, my little one, sleep, sleep.

The little boat rocks in the cove no more,
   But the flying sea-gulls wail;
I peer through the darkness that wraps the shore
   For sight of a home set sail.
     Heave ho, weave low,
       Waves of the briny deep;
     Seethe low and breathe low,
       But sleep you, my little one, sleep, sleep.

Ay, lad of mine, thy father may die
   In the gale that rides the sea,
But we'll not believe it, not you and I,
   Who mind us of Galilee.
     Heave ho, weave low,
       Waves of the briny deep;
     Seethe low and breathe low,
       But sleep you, my little one, sleep, sleep.

Little brown baby wif spa'klin' eyes,
    Come to yo' pappy an' set on his knee.
What you been doin', suh—makin' san' pies?
    Look at dat bib—you's ez du'ty ez me.
Look at dat mouf—dat's merlasses, I bet;
    Come hyeah, Maria, an' wipe off his han's.
Bees gwine to ketch you an' eat you up yit,
    Bein' so sticky an' sweet—goodness lan's!

Little brown baby wif spa'klin' eyes,
    Who's pappy's darlin' an' who's pappy's chile?
Who is it all de day nevah once tries
    Fu' to be cross, er once loses dat smile?
Whah did you git dem teef? My, you's a scamp!
    Whah did dat dimple come f'om in yo' chin?
Pappy do' know you—I b'lieves you's a tramp;
    Mammy, dis hyeah's some ol 'straggler got in!

Let's th'ow him outen de do' in de san',
    We do' want stragglers a-layin' 'roun' hyeah;
Let's gin him 'way to de big buggah-man;
    I know he's hidin' erroun' hyeah right neah.
Buggah-man, buggah-man, come in de do',
    Hyeah's a bad boy, you kin have fu' to eat.
Mammy an' pappy do 'want him no mo',
    Swaller him down f'om his haid to his feet!

Dah, now, I t'ought dat you'd hug me up close.
    Go back, ol' buggah, you sha'n't have dis boy.
He ain't no tramp, ner no straggler, of co'se;
    He's pappy's pa'dner an' playmate an' joy.
Come to you' pallet now—go to yo' res';
    Wisht you could allus know ease an' cleah skies;
Wisht you could stay jes' a chile on my breas'—
    Little brown baby wif spa'klin eyes!

THE SAND-MAN

I know a man
With face of tan,
But who is ever kind;
    Whom girls and boys
    Leave games and toys
Each eventide to find.

    When day grows dim,
    They watch for him,
He comes to place his claim;
    He wears the crown
    Of Dreaming-town;
The sand-man is his name.

    When sparkling eyes
    Troop sleepywise
And busy lips grow dumb;
    When little heads
    Nod toward the beds,
We know the sand-man's come.

II

1 5 6

The light was on the golden sands,
   A glimmer on the sea;
My soul spoke clearly to thy soul,
   Thy spirit answered me.

Since then the light that gilds the sands,
   And glimmers on the sea,
But vainly struggles to reflect
   The radiant soul of thee.

III

The sea speaks to me of you
    All the day long;
Still as I sit by its side
    You are its song.

The sea sings to me of you
    Loud on the reef;
Always it moans as it sings,
    Voicing my grief.

V

There are brilliant heights of sorrow
    That only the few may know;
And the lesser woes of the world, like waves,
    Break noiselessly, far below.
I hold for my own possessing,
    A mount that is lone and still—
The great high place of a hopeless grief,
    And I call it my "Heart-break Hill."
And once on a winter's midnight
    I found its highest crown,
And there in the gloom, my soul and I,
    Weeping, we sat us down.

But now when I seek that summit
    We are two ghosts that go;
Only two shades of a thing that died,
    Once in the long ago.
So I sit me down in the silence,
    And say to my soul, "Be still,"
So the world may not know we died that night,
    From weeping on "Heart-break Hill."

THE MASTER-PLAYER

An old, worn harp that had been played
Till all its strings were loose and frayed,
Joy, Hate, and Fear, each one essayed,
To play. But each in turn had found
No sweet responsiveness of sound.

Then Love the Master-Player came
With heaving breast and eyes aflame;
The Harp he took all undismayed,
Smote on its strings, still strange to song,
And brought forth music sweet and strong.

TO A LADY PLAYING THE HARP

Thy tones are silver melted into sound,
   And as I dream
I see no walls around,
   But seem to hear
   A gondolier
Sing sweetly down some slow Venetian stream.

Italian skies—that I have never seen—
   I see above.
(Ah, play again, my queen;
   Thy fingers white
   Fly swift and light
And weave for me the golden mesh of love.)

Oh, thou dusk sorceress of the dusky eyes
   And soft dark hair,
'T is thou that mak'st my skies
   So swift to change
   To far and strange;
But far and strange, thou still dost make them fair.

Now thou dost sing, and I am lost in thee
   As one who drowns
In floods of melody.
   Still in thy art
   Give me this part,
Till perfect love, the love of loving crowns.

TO A CAPTIOUS CRITIC

Dear critic, who my lightness so deplores,
Would I might study to be prince of bores,
Right wisely would I rule that dull estate—
But, sir, I may not, till you abdicate.

A CHOICE

They please me not—these solemn songs
That hint of sermons covered up.
'T is true the world should heed its wrongs,
    But in a poem let me sup,
Not simples brewed to cure or ease
Humanity's confessed disease,
But the spirit-wine of a singing line,
    Or a dew-drop in a honey cup!

THE POET

He sang of life, serenely sweet,
    With, now and then, a deeper note.
    From some high peak, nigh yet remote,
He voiced the world's absorbing beat.

He sang of love when earth was young,
    And Love, itself, was in his lays.
    But ah, the world, it turned to praise
A jingle in a broken tongue.

Index of Titles

166

Index of First Lines